NO CHOLESTEROL
PASSOVER RECIPES

ALSO BY DEBRA WASSERMAN

The Lowfat Jewish Vegetarian Cookbook

Simply Vegan
(With Reed Mangels, Ph.D., R.D.)

Meatless Meals for Working People
(With Charles Stahler)

NO CHOLESTEROL PASSOVER RECIPES

By Debra Wasserman

The Vegetarian Resource Group
Baltimore, Maryland

A NOTE TO THE READER

The contents of *No Cholesterol Passover Recipes* are not intended to provide personal medical advice. Medical advice should be obtained from a qualified health professional.

© Copyright 1986, revised 1995, Debra Wasserman
Illustrations by Janet Steinberg
Published by The Vegetarian Resource Group,
PO Box 1463, Baltimore, Maryland 21203.

Library of Congress Cataloging-in-Publication Data
No Cholesterol Passover Recipes/Debra Wasserman
Library of Congress Catalog Card Number: 94-61632

ISBN 0-931411-14-9

Printed in the United States of America
10 9 8 7 6 5 4 3 2

CONTENTS

PREFACE

About ten years ago I began to develop vegetarian Passover recipes that contained neither eggs nor dairy products. I glanced through traditional Jewish cookbooks and found an abundance of recipes containing both of these products. Sure the dishes might taste great, but they were also full of cholesterol and fat, items that many people are trying to avoid today. Eating foods containing all this cholesterol and fat is contrary to the dietary guidelines put out by governmental agencies, as well as the American Heart Association and the American Cancer Society. I felt that there was a need to develop alternative healthy Passover recipes and immediately went to work.

First, I spoke to relatives and friends. Some laughed when they heard what I was doing. They felt that it was an impossible task. Others were extremely helpful and encouraging. They shared their own recipes with me and some of them appear in this book.

Secondly, I visited Kosher grocery stores on the Lower East Side in New York City. I mentioned my project and asked for input from some store owners. Most were not concerned with health issues, but enjoyed conversing with me. They eagerly pointed out the Kosher for Passover items they sold in their stores and suggested I use them in my recipes. I then told them that many contained eggs or other animal products. The wife of one store owner said she had many original Passover recipe ideas and was anxious to share them with me. They too, however, contained six to eight eggs in each dish. So, I was more or less going to have to experiment on my own to create these new recipes.

A few minor problems were encountered. First, of course, is that so many foods are already restricted during Passover. Add eggs and dairy products to this list and the task becomes seemingly further impossible. Secondly, even though I live in a city, it was often difficult to find Passover items other than at Passover time itself. Often I had to search for items, but the extra effort was well worth the results.

Through trial and error recipes were created. At times I simply would give up after three or four failures and then would ask a friend to try the same recipe with minor alterations. Perseverance paid off most of the time. I then served many of these new recipes during Passover, as well as other days of the year. Overwhelmingly people were both amazed and pleased with the dishes.

I would especially like to thank my mother and grandmother for teaching me terrific cooking tips. Their basic philosophy is don't be afraid to experiment with foods. My grandmother has never used a measuring cup and my mother always introduced me to new foods. Special thanks also goes to Reed Mangels, Ph.D., R.D., for her nutrition advice, Janet Steinberg for her beautiful illustrations, and to Cindy Blum, Charles Stahler, and Ruth Stahler for contributing recipes to this book. Indeed, it is now possible to celebrate both a happy and _healthy_ Passover.

Debra Wasserman
Baltimore, Maryland
January 1995

(Please note: For those on special diets, please see page 86 before you start using the recipes in this book.)

INTRODUCTION

Inherent in the Jewish spirit is charity, kindness and fighting evil in the world. The core of our lives is to make the earth a better place. Thus keeping Kosher is often said to be Judaism's compromise with its ideal, vegetarianism. In the Garden of Eden, Judaism's depiction of Utopia, man was commanded to be vegetarian (Genesis 1:28-29). The future Kingdom of G-d on earth is also depicted as one in which all creatures will be vegetarian (Isaiah 11:7f).

Tradition

The Jewish religion is a living, breathing organism. While preserving both the law of Torah, and tradition, the Rabbis throughout the centuries have argued, discussed and developed new oral law and customs that both kept the sanctity of the Torah, yet dealt with present reality. This is why the Jewish religion has survived so long.

To eat unleavened bread and to have no form of leaven in the house is the commandment of Passover for all times. Rabbis interpret and enforce this commandment in different ways. For example, to prevent a large economic loss, it was enacted that a Jew could sell the leaven to a non-Jew even though it was not moved to a different property. Jews of eastern European origin generally do not eat corn, beans, legumes or soy products. Sephardic Jews have different daily customs and follow other traditions, for example eating rice. Many Israelis put sesame seeds in their charoset. Settlers in Israel who moved from northern European countries had to form a diet more suitable to the region, thus using more salads, uncooked vegetables, etc.

Consult Your Rabbit

Because there are different traditions, customs and interpretations, you should consult your Rabbi concerning Passover foods. For ethical reasons, we do not use dairy products or eggs. You may of course add these items to your meals or substitute with these foods. However, remember only ANIMAL PRODUCTS OR BY-PRODUCTS CONTAIN CHOLESTEROL!

The Seder Plate

The Pascal lamb was a sacrifice at the time of the Temple, but is no longer required after the destruction of the Sanctuary. Instead of the shankbone, you may want to use a mushroom which has a fleshy texture. The Talmud suggests a broiled beet as an alternative. Many vegans use a potato or an avocado seed in place of the egg.

Vegetarian Passover Recipes

In these recipes, we excluded corn, legumes, etc. since these are not acceptable to the majority of Jews who follow traditional Western dietary patterns. A special problem was presented since many products we could theoretically use are not readily available in certified Kosher for Passover packages. For example, there are commercial candies sold with carob, but as far as we know, carob powder is not available. Potato flour and many spices are other cases. We noticed there is an egg barley and egg noodle product, but none without eggs. In addition, most Kosher for Passover packaged products are high in sodium and contain additives you may not want to use. As the demand increases, more "natural" products will become available. Afterall, many Passover foods now available were not around twenty years ago.

BREAKFASTS

MATZO MEAL PANCAKES
(Makes 8 small pancakes)

For variety, add other fruit to pancake batter including blueberries, finely chopped apples, and raisins. Children will enjoy these pancakes.

3 small ripe bananas, peeled
1/2 cup matzo meal
3/4 cup water
2 teaspoons oil

Mash bananas in a small bowl. Add water and matzo meal. Mix well. Heat oil in a frying pan over medium heat. Form 8 small pancakes in heated pan and fry for about 10 minutes total until brown on both sides.

Total calories per pancake: 72   Fat: 1 gram
Protein: 1 gram   Carbohydrates: 14 grams

EGGLESS SWEET MATZO BRIE
(Serves 4-6)

This dish is delicious served with applesauce or other cooked fruit. Serve in moderation if you're on a restricted lowfat diet.

1 cup nut milk (see beverages)
2 ripe bananas, peeled
1/4 teaspoon cinnamon
8 pieces of matzo
2 teaspoons oil

Place nut milk, bananas, and cinnamon in a blender cup and blend for one minute. Break matzo into 3" x 3" pieces and soak matzo in liquid mixture for 3 minutes. Fry soaked matzo in oiled frying pan over medium heat until brown on each side. Serve warm.

Total calories per serving: 353   Fat: 7 grams
Protein: 8 grams   Carbohydrates: 66 grams

FRUIT SALAD
(Serves 6)

This makes a beautiful centerpiece on any table.

One fresh ripe pineapple
4 pieces of fruit including apples, bananas, and/or pears

Stand pineapple upright and cut in half vertically. Carve out pineapple into bite size pieces. Cut up additional fruit into small pieces. Mix all the fruit together and pour back into pineapple shell. Serve chilled.

Total calories per serving: 49   Fat: 1 gram
Protein: 1 gram   Carbohydrates: 25 grams

PASSOVER MUFFINS
(Makes 6)

Start your morning off with one of these muffins and fresh fruit. Serve the muffins in moderation if you're on a lowfat diet.

2 ripe bananas, peeled
1/2 cup water
1 cup matzo meal
1 carrot, peeled and grated
2/3 cup shredded coconut
1 large apple, peeled and grated

Pre-heat oven to 375 degrees. Mash bananas in a large mixing bowl. Add water, matzo meal, grated carrot, shredded coconut, and grated apple. Divide batter to fit into 6 oiled cupcake tins. Bake 45 minutes at 375 degrees. Completely cool muffins in tins before removing.

Total calories per muffin: 196   Fat: 6 grams
Protein: 3 grams   Carbohydrates: 34 grams

GRANOLA
(Serves 12)

Serve this treat in moderation.

3 cups matzo farfel
1/2 cup each shredded coconut and chopped nuts
1/4 cup oil
1/3 cup sugar or other sweetener
1/4 teaspoon salt
1 teaspoon cinnamon
Grated orange peel to taste
1 cup raisins or other chopped dried fruit

Pre-heat oven to 350 degrees. Combine farfel, coconut and nuts in a large bowl. Spread onto non-stick cookie sheet. Bake 20 minutes at 350 degrees, tossing several times.

Meanwhile, in 2-quart saucepan combine oil, sweetener and salt. Simmer, stirring constantly. Add farfel-coconut-nut mixture. Stir till coated evenly. Add cinnamon and grated orange peel. Spread onto non-stick cookie sheet. Bake 20 minutes at 350 degrees, stirring frequently till brown. Remove and cool. Add raisins. Break up any large chunks with spatula. Store in closed container in the refrigerator until served.

Total calories per serving: 217   Fat: 9 grams
Protein: 2 grams   Carbohydrates: 35 grams

HOME FRIED POTATOES
(Serves 6)

For variety, use sweet potatoes and substitute raisins for the green pepper.

6 potatoes, sliced thinly
1 green pepper, diced finely (optional)
1 onion, chopped finely
Pepper, salt, and paprika to taste
2 teaspoons oil

Place ingredients in frying pan over medium heat. Stir once in a while.
Remove from heat when potatoes are soft and brown, about 20 minutes.

Total calories per serving: 239   Fat: 2 grams
Protein: 5 grams   Carbohydrates: 52 grams

APPLESAUCE
(Serves 6)

This applesauce is terrific served alone or along with pancakes or matzo brie.
As an option, you can also add raisins.

6 apples, diced finely
1 Tablespoon cinnamon
2 oranges, peeled, sectioned, and seeds removed
Water

Place apples, cinnamon, and oranges in a large pot. Cover mixture with water. Cook over medium heat until apples are very soft. Remove from heat and stir well. For a finer consistency blend in blender or food processor.

Total calories per serving: 102   Fat: 1 gram
Protein: 1 gram   Carbohydrates: 26 grams

APPLE LATKES
(Makes 8)

Serve these pancakes with applesauce.

**4 apples, grated
6 Tablespoons matzo meal
1/2 teaspoon cinnamon
2 Tablespoons oil**

Mix apples, matzo meal, and cinnamon together in a bowl. Spoon mixture into oiled frying pan and cook over medium heat for a few minutes. Flip over and cook a few more minutes on the other side.

Total calories per latke: 95   Fat: 4 grams
Protein: 1 gram   Carbohydrates: 16 grams

BEVERAGES

BLENDED FRUIT DRINK
(Serves 4)

Children will absolutely love these fruit shakes.

1 quart orange juice, chilled
2 ripe bananas, peeled
1 cup chopped fruit (apples, pears, strawberries, blue-
    berries, peaches, etc.)

Place ingredients in a blender cup. Blend at high speed for 3 minutes
then serve.

Total calories per serving: 180   Fat: 1 gram
Protein: 3 grams   Carbohydrates: 44 grams

HOT APPLE JUICE

(Serves 8)

Another variation of this recipe is to substitute grape juice for apple juice and orange slices for the lemon slices.

64 ounces apple juice
1 fresh lemon, sliced and seeds removed
Cinnamon to taste

In large pot heat juice, lemon slices and cinnamon over low heat. Stir occasionally. Serve hot.

Total calories per serving: 116   Fat: <1 gram
Protein: <1 gram   Carbohydrates: 29 grams

MELON SHAKE

(Serves 4)

Enjoy these unusual shakes!

1 large ripe cantaloupe, rind and seeds removed and
chopped
1-1/2 cups fruit juice (orange, apple, etc.)

Place melon in blender and add fruit juice slowly while blending at high speed for 2 minutes. For thick shake add less juice.

Total calories per serving: 88   Fat: <1 gram
Protein: 2 grams   Carbohydrates: 21 grams

QUICK CASHEW NUT MILK

(Makes 4 Cups)

Try this unique sweet tasting nut milk in moderation.

1 cup raw cashews
3 cups water

Blend both ingredients together for 5 minutes and refrigerate. Use as beverage or in recipes calling for milk. Shake well before using.

Total calories per 1/2 cup serving: 94   Fat: 8 grams
Protein: 3 grams   Carbohydrates: 5 grams

EASY ALMOND NUT MILK

(Makes about 1-1/2 Cups)

Here's another terrific nut milk. This should be used in moderation, too.

1/2 cup whole, unsalted almonds
1-1/2 cups boiling water

Blend almonds and boiling water together in a blender for about 3 minutes at a high speed. Strain through muslin or cheesecloth. The remaining pulp can be used in vegetable/nut loaves. Shake milk before serving.

Total calories per 1/2 cup serving: 128   Fat: 11 grams
Protein: 4 grams   Carbohydrates: 4 grams

"MILK" SHAKE
(Makes 3 Cups)

This shake is filling. Serve in moderation.

2 cups nut milk (see recipes above), chilled
2 large ripe bananas, peeled
3 Tablespoons cocoa

Blend above ingredients together in a blender at a high speed for 2 minutes before serving.

Total calories per cup serving: 229   Fat: 12 grams
Protein: 6 grams   Carbohydrates: 33 grams

SALADS

SWEET RAINBOW DELIGHT
(Serves 6)

This salad not only tastes great but is quite eye appealing.

3 apples, peeled and grated
2 carrots, peeled and grated
1/3 cup shredded coconut
1/2 cup raisins or other dried fruit, chopped
1/4 cup chopped walnuts

Toss ingredients together in a bowl and serve.

Total calories per serving: 138   Fat: 5 grams
Protein: 2 grams   Carbohydrates: 24 grams

STUFFED TOMATO SALAD
(Serves 4)

Serve stuffed tomatoes with your favorite no-fat dressing.

4 large tomatoes
1 cucumber, diced finely
1/2 cup olives (black or green), chopped
2 stalks celery, chopped
1/2 bunch scallions, finely chopped
1 Tablespoon parsley, finely chopped
Salt and pepper to taste

Scoop out pulp from tomatoes. Mix remaining ingredients together and stuff into tomatoes. Serve chilled.

Total calories per serving: 68   Fat: 3 grams
Protein: 2 grams   Carbohydrates: 11 grams

CUCUMBER SALAD
(Serves 6)

Enjoy this easy salad.

3 cucumbers, sliced thinly
1/2 cup vinegar
1 small onion, chopped finely
Pepper to taste

Mix ingredients together. This can be served immediately, however, the longer it marinates in the refrigerator, the better it will taste.

Total calories per serving: 20   Fat: <1 gram
Protein: 1 gram   Carbohydrates: 5 grams

BEET SALAD
(Serves 6)

For variety, use raw sweet potatoes instead of beets. You can also add crushed pineapple or other fruit. Serve this salad in moderation.

2 beets, peeled and grated
1/2 large head of cabbage, shredded
3 carrots, peeled and grated
Handful of raisins
1 apple, diced
1/4 cup lemon juice
1/4 cup oil
1/4 cup water

Toss ingredients into bowl and mix.

Total calories per serving: 168   Fat: 9 grams
Protein: 2 grams   Carbohydrates: 21 grams

MOLDED VEGETABLE SALAD
(Serves 8)

This salad is a perfect centerpiece on any table.

1 package Kosher for Passover vegetarian gelatin
2/3 cup chopped walnuts
1/2 cup chopped celery
1/2 cup carrots, peeled and shredded
2 small chopped apples, seeds removed

Prepare gelatin as per directions. Before refrigerating blend in other ingredients. Chill in bowl or mold before serving.

Total calories per serving: 164   Fat: 6 grams
Protein: 4 grams   Carbohydrates: 25 grams

TOMATO SALAD
(Serves 4)

Try this quick and easy salad.

4 tomatoes, cut in 1/2-inch wedges
1/3 cup clear vegetable broth
1 teaspoon lemon juice
2 cloves garlic, peeled and minced
Pepper and salt to taste

Mix ingredients together in a bowl and serve.

Total calories per serving: 34   Fat: 1 gram
Protein: 2 grams   Carbohydrates: 7 grams

ORANGE AND ONION SALAD
(Serves 4)

This unique salad blends onions with fresh orange slices.

1 onion, peeled and sliced into rings
1/3 small head lettuce
6 large oranges, peeled, sliced, and seeds removed
1 Tablespoon fresh parsley, chopped

Soak onion rings in a bowl of ice water for several hours. Arrange lettuce on a platter. Place a layer of oranges on it and top with drained onion rings. Garnish with parsley.

Total calories per serving: 127   Fat: <1 gram
Protein: 3 grams   Carbohydrates: 31 grams

CRANBERRY SALAD
(Serves 12)

Fresh cranberry salad tastes so much better than the canned variety.

12 ounces fresh cranberries
1/2 cup orange juice or apple juice
1 cup raisins
1 cup shredded coconut
2 stalks celery, chopped finely
1 apple, chopped finely
2/3 cup chopped walnuts (optional)

Place cranberries, juice, and raisins in a blender cup and blend together for 3 minutes. Pour mixture into a bowl and add the remaining ingredients. Stir well, chill, and serve.

Total calories per serving: 110   Fat: 4 grams
Protein: 4 grams   Carbohydrates: 19 grams

PICKLED BEETS
(Serves 4-6)

This salad needs to be marinated before serving.

One 16-ounce can sliced beets or equivalent fresh, cooked and sliced
3/4 cup vinegar
1/4 cup water
1 onion, sliced into rings
Salt and sugar to taste (optional)

Mix vinegar, water, salt and sugar together in large jar. Add beets and onions. Place in refrigerator for 1 day or until ready to serve.

Total calories per serving: 40   Fat: <1 gram
Protein: 1 gram   Carbohydrates: 10 grams

ZUCCHINI AND TOMATO SALAD
(Serves 4-6)

Enjoy this delicious, lowfat salad.

2 small zucchini, sliced
3 tomatoes, chopped or sliced
1 small onion, sliced and separated into rings
1 Tablespoon lemon juice
Salt, pepper, and fresh minced parsley to taste
1/2 cup black olives or walnuts, chopped (optional)

Toss ingredients in a bowl. Refrigerate at least one hour before serving. May be served plain or with no-fat salad dressing.

Total calories per serving: 41   Fat: <1 gram
Protein: 2 grams   Carbohydrates: 9 grams

POTATO SALAD AND OLIVES
(Serves 6)

Enjoy this hearty salad in moderation!

5 large potatoes, cubed into small pieces
3 stalks of celery, diced
3 carrots, peeled and chopped

1 onion, chopped finely
1/4 cup black olives, drained and sliced
3 Tablespoons mayonnaise (see recipe on next page)
Salt and pepper to taste

Cook potatoes till soft. Allow them to cool. Mix in remaining
ingredients with potatoes. Garnish with parsley.

Total calories per serving: 270   Fat: 7 grams
Protein: 5 grams   Carbohydrates: 49 grams

DRESSINGS

CINDY'S EGGLESS MAYONNAISE
(Makes 1-1/2 Cups)

Try this unique almond-based mayonnaise. Use in moderation.

1/2 cup raw almonds
1-1/2 cups boiling water
1 cup oil
Juice of one lemon
1 teaspoon vinegar
1 teaspoon white horseradish
1/4 teaspoon garlic powder

Blend almonds and boiling water together for about three minutes. Strain through cheesecloth or muslin.

Pour 1/2 cup of this "almond milk" and 1/2 cup oil into blender. As you blend at high speed, slowly drizzle in the remaining oil. It should start to thicken. Then add the other ingredients and blend one more minute until the consistency of mayonnaise.

WARNING: THIS RECIPE WILL NOT WORK ON A DAMP, HUMID, OR RAINY DAY!

Total calories per 1 Tablespoon serving: 86   Fat: 10 grams
Protein: <1 gram   Carbohydrates: 1 gram

SWEET FRENCH DRESSING
(Makes 2 Cups)

This dressing is delicious served with romaine lettuce and sliced tomatoes.

1/3 cup oil
2/3 cup orange juice
2 oranges, peeled and seeds removed
2 Tablespoons lemon juice
1 Tablespoon vinegar
1 teaspoon salt
1 teaspoon paprika
Slice of small onion, minced

Blend all ingredients at high speed for 3 minutes.
Chill and serve with favorite salad.

Total calories per 2 Tablespoons serving: 49   Fat: 4 grams
Protein: <1 gram   Carbohydrates: 3 grams

GUACAMOLE
(Makes 1-1/2 Cups)

Spread this dressing on matzo for a delicious snack, too.

1 large ripe avocado, seed and skin removed
1 large tomato, finely chopped
1 teaspoon lemon juice
Pepper and salt to taste

Mash avocado in a bowl. Add chopped tomato, lemon juice, and seasonings. Mix well. Serve over salad or with raw veggies.

Total calories per 2 Tablespoons serving: 35   Fat: 3 grams
Protein: <1 gram   Carbohydrates: 2 grams

RUSSIAN SALAD DRESSING
(Makes 1-2/3 Cups)

This dressing combines fresh tomatoes with lemon juice and a touch of horseradish.

4 large ripe tomatoes
1/4 cup oil
1/4 cup water
1/4 cup lemon juice
1 small onion, minced finely
1 teaspoon each salt, horseradish, and paprika
1 clove garlic, peeled and minced

Place all ingredients in a blender cup and blend together for 3 minutes.

Total calories per 2 Tablespoons serving: 51   Fat: 4 grams
Protein: 1 gram   Carbohydrates: 3 grams

LEMON/APPLE GARLIC DRESSING
(Makes 3 Cups)

Enjoy this fat-free salad dressing!

1 cup vinegar
1-1/2 cups water
2 Tablespoons lemon juice
2 cloves garlic, peeled and minced
1/4 teaspoon each pepper and salt
1 apple, cored and chopped

Blend all ingredients together for 3 minutes.

Total calories per 2 Tablespoons serving: 5   Fat: 0 grams
Protein: 0 grams   Carbohydrates: 2 grams

RED BEET DRESSING
(Makes 2 Cups)

Savor this slightly sweet dressing!

1 beet, peeled and chopped
1-1/4 cups orange juice
1/4 cup oil
1 clove garlic, peeled and minced
Salt to taste

Place all the ingredients in a blender cup and blend for 3 minutes.

Total calories per 2 Tablespoons serving: 43   Fat: 3 grams
Protein: <1 gram   Carbohydrates: 3 grams

SOUPS

CARROT CREAM SOUP
(Serves 6)

This pureed soup is absolutely terrific! If you don't puree the mixture it also makes an excellent vegetarian soup stock.

1 pound carrots, peeled and chopped
1 onion, chopped
1 Tablespoon oil plus 3 Tablespoons water
6 cups water
Salt and pepper to taste
1/3 cup fresh parsley, chopped finely

In three quart pot sauté the chopped onions and carrots in the oil and water mixture for 10 minutes over a medium heat. Add 6 cups water and seasonings. Bring to a boil. Reduce heat, cover, and simmer for 20 minutes. Puree in blender, return mixture to pot, and reheat before serving.

Total calories per serving: 60   Fat: 2 grams
Protein: 1 gram   Carbohydrates: 9 grams

POTATO SOUP
(Serves 6)

Enjoy this delicious hearty soup!

4 medium potatoes, cubed into small pieces
1 cup celery, chopped
1 cup carrots, peeled and chopped
1 teaspoon oil
1 medium onion, chopped finely
1/2 cup fresh parsley, chopped
1/2 green pepper, chopped finely
Pepper and paprika to taste
1 Tablespoon potato starch
1 teaspoon oil

Cook chopped potatoes, celery, and carrots for five minutes over medium heat in a pot with about 3 inches of water. Fry onion in oil and add to mixture. Next, add parsley, green pepper, and spices.

Brown potato starch in 1 teaspoon hot oil in a separate pot. Add some of the soup mixture carefully to starch mixture and blend. Then add to soup and cook until vegetables are tender.

Total calories per serving: 119   Fat: 2 grams
Protein: 2 grams   Carbohydrates: 24 grams

ONION SOUP
(Serves 8)

Here's a relatively simple soup to prepare.

6 medium onions, sliced and separated into rings
2 carrots, peeled and sliced thinly
1 pound small mushrooms (optional)
1 or 2 cloves garlic, peeled and minced
3 Tablespoons oil
8 cups water
1 teaspoon lemon juice
Pepper and salt to taste

Sauté onions, carrots, mushrooms and garlic in oil over high heat for about 8 minutes until onions become soft and turn slightly brown. Add water, lemon juice, pepper and salt and continue warming over medium heat until hot.

Total calories per serving: 79   Fat: 5 grams
Protein: 1 gram   Carbohydrates: 8 grams

SWEET POTATO SOUP
(Serves 8)

This is a sweet hearty soup!

3 pounds sweet potatoes, peeled and cubed
3 large carrots, peeled and sliced
2 celery stalks, chopped
6 cups water

2 Tablespoons lemon juice
1 teaspoon paprika
Pepper and salt to taste
1-1/2 cups cashew milk (see beverage section for recipe)

Place sweet potatoes, carrots, and celery in a large pot and cover with water. Cook over medium heat until potatoes are tender. Drain (saving broth for other soups) and mash half of the mixture only.

Pour mashed mixture and remaining cooked veggies into a large pot. Add water, lemon juice, paprika, seasonings, and cashew milk and heat over medium heat until hot. Serve warm.

Total calories per serving: 229   Fat: 3 grams
Protein: 4 grams   Carbohydrates: 47 grams

VEGETABLE SOUP
(Serves 10)

Feel free to substitute other vegetables in this soup such as chopped squash.

1 small onion, chopped
1/4 pound mushrooms, chopped
2 Tablespoons oil
10 cups water
3 stalks celery, chopped
3 carrots, peeled and chopped
2 turnips, peeled and chopped
2 white potatoes, peeled and chopped
1 teaspoon fresh parsley, finely minced
Salt and pepper to taste

Sauté onion and mushrooms in oil. Add the remaining ingredients and simmer for 1 hour. Serve warm.

Total calories per serving: 67   Fat: 3 grams
Protein: 1 gram   Carbohydrates: 10 grams

CREAM OF VEGETABLE SOUP
(Serves 6)

Feel free to substitute different vegetables such as squash and asparagus. If on a lowfat diet, serve this soup in moderation.

2/3 cup whole, unsalted almonds
3 cups boiling water
1 cup water
2 white potatoes, peeled and chopped
2 carrots, peeled and chopped
4 stalks celery, chopped
Pepper, garlic powder and salt to taste

Place almonds and boiling water in a blender cup and blend together for 3 minutes. Strain liquid through muslin or cheesecloth.

Put nutmilk and remaining ingredients in a large pot and bring to a boil. Reduce heat and simmer 30 minutes. Remove from heat and allow to cool for a little while.

Pour mixture into a blender cup and blend till creamy. Pour soup back into a large pot and reheat. Add water to thin soup if desired.

Total calories per serving: 148   Fat: 8 grams
Protein: 4 grams   Carbohydrates: 18 grams

MUSHROOM POTATO SOUP

(Serves 10-12)

This soup can be a meal by itself.

2 medium onions, chopped
2 cloves garlic, peeled and minced
2 stalks celery, diced
1 pound mushrooms, chopped
2 Tablespoons oil
4 small potatoes, cubed
1/2 teaspoon garlic powder
2 teaspoons salt (optional)
1 teaspoon fresh parsley, minced
10 cups water
2 carrots, peeled and diced

Sauté onions, garlic, celery, and mushrooms in oil in a large pot until celery is tender. Add potatoes, seasonings, and water. Bring to a boil. Reduce heat and simmer soup for 45 minutes. Add carrots and simmer 10 minutes longer. Serve warm.

Total calories per serving: 86   Fat: 3 grams
Protein: 2 grams   Carbohydrates: 14 grams

THICK CABBAGE/BEET SOUP
(Serves 10-12)

This is an extremely thick, hearty soup.

2 cups grated beets (about 4 beets)
1/2 small cabbage, shredded
2 carrots, peeled and grated
1/4 cup onions, chopped
1/4 cup celery, chopped
3 Tablespoons lemon juice
12 cups water
1 teaspoon fresh dill, finely minced
1/4 teaspoon paprika

Place all the ingredients in a large pot and cook together over low heat for 45 minutes. Serve soup hot or cold.

Total calories per serving: 25   Fat: <1 gram
Protein: 1 gram   Carbohydrates: 6 grams

FRESH TOMATO SOUP
(Serves 4)

Fresh tomato soup is fantastic!

1 large onion, chopped
5 small ripe tomatoes, chopped
1-1/2 cups water
1/2 teaspoon fresh parsley, minced
Pepper and salt to taste

Combine all the ingredients in a large pot and cook over medium heat for 15 minutes and then cool. Place mixture in a blender cup and blend until creamy. Reheat and serve hot.

Total calories per serving: 32   Fat: <1 gram
Protein: 1 gram   Carbohydrates: 7 grams

CHOW MEIN NOODLES
(Serves 10-12)

Enjoy these homemade chow mein noodles in your soup.

**1/2 cup matzo meal
2 Tablespoons potato starch
Just under 2/3 cup water**

Mix the ingredients together and refrigerate dough for 15 minutes.
    Preheat oven to 400 degrees. Remove dough from refrigerator and divide into 2 balls. Flatten balls of dough on a board covered with some matzo meal. Sprinkle some matzo meal on rolling pin and roll out dough until 1/8 inch thick. Slice into thin strips or wider strips if desired. Bake at 400 degrees for 15 minutes until light brown and crunchy. Serve with any type of soup.

Total calories per serving: 32   Fat: <1 gram
Protein: 1 gram   Carbohydrates: 7 grams

SOUP NUTS
(Makes about 18)

Add these to any soup.

1/4 cup matzo meal
1 Tablespoon potato starch
just under 1/3 cup water

Mix ingredients together to form a ball of smooth dough. You may have to add a little more water. Refrigerate for 15 minutes.

Preheat oven to 400 degrees. Remove dough from refrigerator and roll into small 1/2 inch diameter balls. Place on lightly oiled baking sheet and bake for 35 minutes at 400 degrees. For smoother looking soup nuts, toss them into a pot of boiling water for 1/2 minute before baking.

Total calories per nut: 9   Fat: 0 grams
Protein: <1 gram   Carbohydrates: 2 grams

SIDE DISHES

PRUNE AND POTATO TSIMMES
(Serves 8)

This slow-cooked dish is well worth the wait.

1/2 cup diced onions
2 teaspoons oil
2 pounds white potatoes, peeled and chopped
1-1/4 teaspoons salt (optional)
2-1/2 cups liquid from prunes and water
1 teaspoon paprika
1 Tablespoon lemon juice
1 small jar stewed prunes (approximately 16 ounces)

In a 4-quart saucepan, sauté onions in oil over medium heat until soft. Put potatoes, salt, prune juice and water, paprika, and lemon juice in pot with onions. Simmer uncovered over low heat for 1-1/4 hours. Add drained prunes and cook 1/2 hour longer stirring occasionally. Serve warm.

Total calories per serving: 172   Fat: 1 gram
Protein: 3 grams   Carbohydrates: 40 grams

POTATO PANCAKES

(Serves 6)

Serve this dish with applesauce or other cooked fruit.

3 cups potatoes (about 3-4)
1 onion, finely chopped
Pepper and salt to taste
Handful fresh parsley, finely chopped (optional)
1 Tablespoon oil

Cook potatoes in water until tender and mash or grate raw potatoes. Place in large bowl and add onion and seasonings. Mix well. Form six pancakes in a large oiled pan over medium heat and fry until lightly browned on each side.

Total calories per serving: 93   Fat: 3 grams
Protein: 2 grams   Carbohydrates: 17 grams

ADELE'S EGGPLANT CAVIAR

(Serves 6)

Spread this caviar on matzo.

1 large eggplant
2 large tomatoes, chopped
1 clove garlic, peeled and minced
2 Tablespoons olive oil
1 green pepper, seeds removed and chopped
1 large onion, chopped finely
2 Tablespoons dry wine or vinegar
Pepper and salt to taste

Preheat oven to 350 degrees. Prick eggplant with a fork. Place in a pan and bake eggplant with skin for 1 hour at 350 degrees. Remove baked eggplant from oven and allow to cool. Peel eggplant and chop. Mix eggplant with tomatoes.

While eggplant is baking, sauté garlic in oil. Add green pepper and onion and sauté until tender. Add eggplant and tomatoes. Add wine and seasonings. Mix thoroughly and cook until thick. Cool in refrigerator for at least 1 hour before serving.

Total calories per serving: 82   Fat: 5 grams
Protein: 1 gram   Carbohydrates: 9 grams

SWEET AND SOUR CABBAGE
(Serves 6-8)

Try this creative cabbage dish.

1 small head cabbage (red and/or green), core removed and
    shredded
1 onion, chopped
2 Tablespoons oil
1/2 cup raisins
1 apple, cored and grated
1 cup water
1 Tablespoon matzo meal
2 Tablespoons vinegar
1 Tablespoon sugar or other sweetener
2 teaspoons salt

Sauté cabbage and onions in oil in a large pot over medium heat. Add raisins, grated apple, and 1/2 C water. Simmer 5 minutes.

In jar shake up matzo meal, vinegar, sweetener, salt, and 1/2 C water.
Add to other ingredients in pot and cook 10 minutes longer. Serve warm.

Total calories per serving: 131   Fat: 5 grams
Protein: 2 grams   Carbohydrates: 23 grams

SWEET POTATO/FRUIT CASSEROLE
(Serves 8)

For variety use different types of fresh and dried fruit in this casserole.

8 sweet potatoes, peeled and thinly sliced
4 apples, cored and thinly sliced
4 pears, cored and thinly sliced
1 cup raisins
1/3 cup nuts (optional)
1 Tablespoon lemon juice
1 teaspoon cinnamon
2 teaspoons oil

Place sweet potatoes in a large baking pan, alternating with apple and pear
slices. Scatter with raisins (and chopped nuts if you desire) as you form
layers. Sprinkle dish with lemon juice, cinnamon and oil. Cover and
bake casserole at 350 degrees for about 1 hour till tender. Serve warm.

Total calories per serving: 278   Fat: 2 grams
Protein: 3 grams   Carbohydrates: 67 grams

STUFFED MUSHROOMS 1
(Serves 3)

Serve this dish as an appetizer.

6 very large fresh mushrooms
1 Tablespoon finely chopped onion
2 teaspoons oil
1/4 cup vegetable broth
3/4 cup matzo farfel
Pepper and salt to taste
2 Tablespoons red wine (or tomato juice)
2 Tablespoons water

Carefully remove stems from mushrooms and chop them finely. Sauté the stems and onion in oil in a large frying pan over medium heat for 5 minutes. Remove from heat and add broth, farfel, and seasonings to sautéed mixture. Mix well.

Preheat oven to 400 degrees. Arrange mushroom caps in a 6 X 10 inch baking pan cap side up. Fill with stuffing. Mix red wine or tomato juice and water together and spoon evenly over mushrooms. Bake 15 minutes at 400 degrees. Serve warm.

Total calories per serving: 125   Fat: 4 grams
Protein: 2 grams   Carbohydrates: 20 grams

STUFFED MUSHROOMS II
(Serves 6)

These stuffed mushrooms are best served chilled.

12 large mushrooms
1/4 cup vegetable broth
1 small ripe avocado, seed removed
1 ripe tomato, diced
Pinch of pepper and garlic powder

Remove stems from mushrooms and discard. Sauté mushrooms in broth for 3 minutes. Remove from heat and cool. Mash avocado. Add tomato and spices. Mix well and stuff mushrooms. Refrigerate before serving.

Total calories per serving: 59   Fat: 4 grams
Protein: 2 grams   Carbohydrates: 5 grams

CARROTS 'N' GINGER
(Serves 6-8)

Fresh ginger and carrots taste wonderful together.

1 pound carrots, cut lengthwise into 1-inch thin strips
1 inch fresh ginger, diced finely
1 cup water
Salt to taste (optional)

Bake together in dish for 1 hour at 400 degrees.

Total calories per serving: 33   Fat: <1 gram
Protein: 1 gram   Carbohydrates: 8 grams

VEGETABLE BAKE
(Serves 6)

Substitute different vegetables in this dish for variety.

1/2 pound (8 ounces) broccoli, chopped
1 medium onion, chopped
1 large carrot, peeled and chopped finely
2 stalks celery, chopped
1/3 cup water
8 ounces tomato sauce
Dash of pepper
1/4 teaspoon garlic powder
1/2 teaspoon fresh parsley, minced
1/2 cup matzo meal

Steam broccoli, onion, carrot, and celery in water for 15 minutes. Add 6 ounces tomato sauce, spices, and matzo meal. Mix well.

Preheat oven to 375 degrees. Press mixture into small casserole dish. Cover with remaining 2 ounces tomato sauce. Bake at 375 degrees for 15 minutes. Serve warm.

Total calories per serving: 79   Fat: <1 gram
Protein: 3 grams   Carbohydrates: 18 grams

STUFFED PEARS
(Serves 6)

This unqiue dish tastes delicious.

3 ripe pears, cut in half lengthwise
2 baked sweet potatoes, peeled and mashed
1/4 teaspoon ginger
1/2 cup raisins
1/4 cup chopped walnuts
2 Tablespoons shredded coconut

Preheat oven to 375 degrees. Scoop out core in each pear half. Mix remaining ingredients well and stuff into pear halves. Bake at 375 degrees for 25 minutes, adding a little water to bottom of pan. Serve warm or chilled.

Total calories per serving: 166   Fat: 4 grams
Protein: 3 grams   Carbohydrates: 33 grams

REED'S FRUIT SPREAD
(Serves 12)

Even very young children will enjoy this sweet spread.

8 ounces mixed dried fruit (apricots, prunes, peaches, etc.)
1 large apple, cored and chopped
1/2 teaspoon cinnamon
2 Tablespoons matzo meal

Place dried fruit in saucepan with enough water to cover fruit. Cook over medium heat until fruit is soft and plump. Cool and place fruit and any remaining cooking liquid in a food processor bowl. Add apples and blend until smooth. Stir in cinnamon and matzo meal. Spread on matzo to serve.

Total calories per serving: 61   Fat: <1 gram
Protein: 1 gram   Carbohydrates: 16 grams

CHOPPED "LIVER" SPREAD
(Makes about 1 cup)

Guests will rave about this mock chopped "liver" spread. If you're on a lowfat diet, serve in moderation.

3 Tablespoons vegetable broth
1/2 pound mushrooms, chopped
1 small onion, chopped
1 cup chopped walnuts
Pepper and salt to taste
1 Tablespoon water

Sauté mushrooms and onion in vegetable broth over medium heat for 8 minutes. Pour mixture into blender or food processor cup, adding walnuts, seasonings and water. Blend until smooth. Serve with matzo as a spread.

Total calories per 2 Tablespoons serving: 107   Fat: 9 grams
Protein: 5 grams   Carbohydrates: 4 grams

POTATO KNISHES
(Makes 8)

Enjoy these knishes for lunch or as a late night snack.

1-1/2 cups matzo meal
1/4 cup potato starch
1-1/3 cups water
1 large onion, chopped
2 teaspoons oil
3 cups cooked and mashed potatoes (about 5)
1/4 teaspoon paprika
1/4 teaspoon pepper
Salt to taste (optional)

Mix matzo meal, starch and water together and refrigerate for 15 minutes. Form into 2 balls. Roll out each ball to 1/4 inch thick, and cut into 3 X 5 inch squares.

Preheat oven to 400 degrees. Sauté onions in oil in a frying pan over medium heat until soft. Mix together sautéed onions, cooked potatoes, and seasonings in a large bowl. Lay about 1-1/2 Tablespoons potato/onion filling in each dough square. Fold in sides and pinch closed. Lay on oiled baking pan. Bake at 400 degrees until light brown. Serve warm.

Total calories per knish: 177   Fat: 2 grams
Protein: 4 grams   Carbohydrates: 37 grams

POTATO/KALE CASSEROLE
(Serves 6-8)

Here's a creative way to serve dark leafy greens.

3 pounds potatoes, cooked and mashed
1 onion, chopped
1 clove garlic, minced (optional)
2 teaspoons oil
1 pound kale, chopped
2 Tablespoons water
Pepper and salt to taste

Pre-cook potatoes and mash. In separate pan sauté onion and garlic in oil over medium heat for 3 minutes. Next add kale and water and steam covered until kale is tender.

Preheat oven to 350 degrees. Remove from heat and mix steamed kale with potatoes and seasonings. Pour into casserole dish and bake at 350 degrees till warmed through before serving.

Total calories per serving: 242   Fat: 2 grams
Protein: 6 grams   Carbohydrates: 51 grams

SWEET POTATO KUGEL

(Serves 12)

Not only does this kugel taste great but it looks beautiful on the table.

6 small sweet potatoes, peeled and grated
3 apples, peeled and grated
1 cup raisins
1 cup matzo meal
2 teaspoon cinnamon
1 cup walnuts, chopped (optional)
1 cup fruit juice or water

Preheat oven to 375 degrees. Mix ingredients together. Press into large baking dish. Bake 45 minutes at 375 degrees until crisp on top. Serve.

Total calories per serving: 156   Fat: <1 gram
Protein: 2 grams   Carbohydrates: 38 grams

BAKED STUFFED ZUCCHINI

(Serves 4)

Although there are a few steps involved in this recipe, it's well worth the effort.

2 medium zucchini, cut lengthwise in half
Small onion, chopped finely
1/4 cup tomato sauce
1/2 teaspoon fresh parsley, minced
1/4 teaspoon garlic powder
2 Tablespoons matzo meal

Scoop out pulp of zucchini halves and chop. Heat pulp, onion, sauce, and spices in a pan over medium heat for 5 minutes. Add matzo meal to mixture and mix well.

Preheat oven to 450 degrees. Restuff zucchini with mixture. Place in baking pan with a little water on bottom. Bake at 450 degrees for 30 minutes until zucchini shells are soft. Serve warm.

Total calories per serving: 50   Fat: <1 gram
Protein: 2 grams   Carbohydrates: 11 grams

BEETS
(Serves 4)

Dill and beets together in one dish are absolutely terrific!

8 small fresh beets, peeled and sliced
1-1/3 cups water
1/2 teaspoon fresh dill, chopped finely
2 Tablespoons lemon juice
1 Tablespoon potato starch dissolved in 1/3 cup water

Cook beets, dill, and lemon juice in water in a small pot over medium heat for 40 minutes. Add potato starch/water mixture. Mix well and heat 5 more minutes in covered pot, stirring often. Serve warm or chilled.

Total calories per serving: 33   Fat: <1 gram
Protein: 1 gram   Carbohydrates: 7 grams

BROCCOLI OR ASPARAGUS AND ALMOND SAUCE

(Serves 4)

Enjoy this dish in moderation.

1/3 cup slivered almonds
2 teaspoons margarine
1/4 cup vegetable broth
1/4 teaspoon salt (optional)
Pinch of pepper
1 teaspoon lemon juice
2 cup cooked asparagus or cooked broccoli, chopped

Sauté almonds in margarine and vegetable broth with seasonings for 5 minutes. Remove from heat and add lemon juice. Pour over cooked broccoli or asparagus and serve warm.

Total calories per serving: 88   Fat: 7 grams
Protein: 4 grams   Carbohydrates: 5 grams

OVEN FRIES
(Serves 6)

Adults and children alike will enjoy these baked fries.

6 potatoes, sliced thin
2 teaspoons oil
Garlic powder, pepper, and salt to taste

Preheat oven to 450 degrees. Place sliced potatoes on lightly oiled non-stick cookie sheet. Drizzle oil and seasonings over them. Bake 5 minutes at 450 degrees. Turn potatoes over and bake another 5 minutes. Serve warm.

Total calories per serving: 233   Fat: 2 grams
Protein: 5 grams   Carbohydrates: 51 grams

TOMATO AND ONION DISH
(Serves 8)

This dish consists of several layers, similar to a lasagna-type dish.

4 onions, sliced
4 cups canned stewed tomatoes
1 teaspoon salt (optional)
1/4 teaspoon pepper
2 Tablespoons sugar or other sweetener
3 matzos
2 Tablespoons margarine

Preheat oven to 375 degrees. Line a 9 X 9 inch baking pan with 1/3 of the slices of onion. In bowl, season tomatoes with salt, pepper and sweetener. Place 1/3 of the tomatoes on top of the onions, then a piece of matzo. Repeat two times ending with the matzo. Dot with margarine. Bake at 375 degrees for 30 minutes. Serve warm.

Total calories per serving: 130   Fat: 3 grams
Protein: 3 grams   Carbohydrates: 25 grams

EASY GRATED POTATO PUDDING
(Serves 6)

This potato kugel is delicious. Serve with a mushroom or onion gravy.

6 medium potatoes (about 2 pounds), peeled
1 large onion
1 large carrot, peeled
1/4 cup matzo meal
1-1/2 teaspoons salt (optional)
1/4 teaspoon pepper
2 Tablespoons vegetable broth
2 Tablespoons oil

Preheat oven to 375 degrees. Grate potatoes, onion and carrots. Add
remaining ingredients. Mix well. Pour into well oiled large baking pan.
Bake at 375 degrees for 1 hour. Serve warm.

Total calories per serving: 242   Fat: 5 grams
Protein: 5 grams   Carbohydrates: 46 grams

ZUCCHINI AND TOMATOES
(Serves 4)

Here's another hearty side dish.

1-1/2 pounds zucchini, chopped
2 large tomatoes, chopped
1/3 cup vegetable broth

1 large clove garlic, minced
2 Tablespoons fresh parsley, finely chopped
1 Tablespoon lemon juice
1 teaspoon paprika

In oil sauté all the ingredients together for about 10 minutes or until the zucchini is tender. Serve warm.

Total calories per serving: 49   Fat: 1 gram
Protein: 3 grams   Carbohydrates: 10 grams

SAUTÉED MUSHROOMS
(Serves 4)

This recipe is simple to prepare.

1 pound mushrooms, chopped
1 large onion, chopped finely
1 Tablespoon oil
2 Tablespoons vegetable broth
Garlic powder, salt and pepper to taste

Sauté the mushrooms and onions in oil and broth. Season to taste. Cook over low heat for about 8 minutes until mushrooms are soft.

Total calories per serving: 73   Fat: 4 grams
Protein: 3 grams   Carbohydrates: 8 grams

MAIN DISHES

SWEET STUFFED CABBAGE 1
(Serves 6-8)

Although this recipe takes some time to prepare, it is well worth the effort.

1 small cabbage
5 sweet potatoes, baked and mashed
1 cup pineapple chunks
2 apples, chopped
3/4 cup raisins
1-1/2 teaspoons cinnamon
1/2 cup walnuts, chopped (optional)
29 ounce can tomato sauce
1 cup water

Steam head of cabbage in pot with water until leaves are soft. Carefully remove whole steamed leaves and set aside.

Preheat oven to 375 degrees. Mix together cooked sweet potatoes, pineapple, apples, raisins, cinnamon, and walnuts, if desired. Place 1/4 cup of mixture on center of each cabbage leaf and fold ends in. Lay in deep baking pan with folded cabbage ends down. Mix tomato sauce with water and pour over cabbage so leaves remain moist. Bake at 375 degrees for 30 minutes. Serve warm.

Total calories per serving: 273   Fat: 1 gram
Protein: 5 grams   Carbohydrates: 67 grams

EGGPLANT PATTIES
(Makes 12)

These pancakes are delicious.

1 large eggplant, peeled and cubed
1/2 cup matzo meal
1 onion, chopped finely
Parsley flakes, garlic powder, pepper, and salt to taste
1 Tablespoon oil
2 cups tomato sauce

Boil peeled eggplant until very soft. Drain and mash in bowl.
Add matzo meal, onion, and spices. Mix well. Form 3 inch patties and fry in oil on both sides over medium heat until light brown. Serve covered with heated tomato sauce.

Total calories per pattie: 64   Fat: 1 gram
Protein: 2 grams   Carbohydrates: 12 grams

STIR FRIED VEGETABLES
(Serves 4)

Feel free to use any variety of vegetables in this dish.

In large frying pan with 2 Tablespoons oil stir fry 6 cups of your favorite chopped veggies including carrots, celery, cauliflower, broccoli, tomatoes, onions, etc. until soft. Season with your favorite herbs. Serve over plain mashed potatoes to reduce the overall fat content of this dish.

Total calories per serving (without mashed potatoes): 127   Fat: 7 grams
Protein: 3 grams   Carbohydrates: 15 grams

CHINESE-STYLE CABBAGE
(Serves 6)

This Chinese dish is absolutely delicious.

1/2 head large cabbage or 1 Chinese cabbage, shredded
1 carrot, peeled and chopped very finely
1/2 bunch scallions, chopped finely
Fresh ginger, grated and salt to taste
1/2 cup water

Sauté all the above ingredients over high heat until cabbage is soft. Stir often. Serve warm.

Total calories per serving: 20   Fat: <1 gram
Protein: 1 gram   Carbohydrates: 5 grams

STUFFED PEPPERS
(Serves 4)

This dish makes a beautiful centerpiece on any dinner table.

4 large green bell peppers
2 teaspoons oil
3/4 cup matzo farfel or 2 pieces of matzo, crushed
1/2 cup raisins
1 stalk celery, chopped
1 carrot, peeled and grated
1 Tablespoon dry red wine or apple juice

Cut off tops of green peppers and take out seeds.

Preheat oven to 350 degrees. Sauté the farfel, raisins, celery, carrot, and wine or juice with oil over medium heat for 10-15 minutes. Stuff peppers with the mixture.

Bake in dish at 350 degrees for 1/2 hour or until peppers are soft. You may want to put some water in the bottom of the pan to prevent peppers from drying out.

Total calories per serving: 166   Fat: 2 grams
Protein: 2 grams   Carbohydrates: 36 grams

POTATO VEGETABLE STEW
(Serves 6)

Enjoy this hearty stew!

2 pounds small potatoes
29 ounce can tomato sauce
Garlic powder, pepper, and salt to taste
4 small tomatoes, cut in 1/2 inch wedges
3 carrots, peeled and diced
3 stalks celery, chopped
12 ounces spinach (1 bag), rinsed and cooked

Boil potatoes in water until tender, drain, and cube into small pieces.

Preheat oven to 350 degrees. Mix seasonings into tomato sauce. Put all ingredients into a bowl and blend well. Pour into a large baking dish. Bake at 350 degrees for 30 minutes, or until vegetables are done. Serve warm.

Total calories per serving: 220   Fat: 1 gram
Protein: 7 grams   Carbohydrates: 51 grams

VEGETABLE NUT LOAF
(Serves 6)

This loaf is served chilled. Eat in moderation.

2 cups carrots, peeled and grated
2 cups celery, chopped finely
1/2 cup cabbage, shredded
1/4 cup vegetable broth
1 ripe avocado, peeled and mashed
1 cup ground nuts (walnuts, almonds, etc.)
1 cup matzo meal
2 Tablespoons fresh parsley, chopped
1 small onion, chopped finely
Pepper and salt to taste

Sauté carrots, celery, and cabbage in broth over high heat for 10 minutes. Add remaining ingredients and mix well. Press into loaf pan. Chill in refrigerator for at least 2 hours. Serve in slices.

Total calories per serving: 250   Fat: 13 grams
Protein: 7 grams   Carbohydrates: 29 grams

NUT "CHEESE" SURPRISE
(Serves 8)

This is a unique Passover dish that should be served in moderation to those on a restricted lowfat diet.

Cheese: 1/2 cup raw cashews
1/2 cup water
1/4 cup lemon juice
1 Tablespoon vegetable broth
2 Tablespoons oil
Garlic powder and paprika to taste
1/2 small ripe tomato, chopped

Preheat oven to 350 degrees. In a blender cup, blend cashews, water, lemon juice, and broth together. Slowly add oil. Then add above remaining ingredients and blend well for 1 minute. Once the "cheese" is made add the ingredients below.

6 potatoes, chopped and cooked
1 onion, chopped
3 carrots, sliced thinly
2 green peppers, chopped finely

Mix well and pour into large baking dish. Bake in oven for 30 minutes at 350 degrees. Serve warm.

Total calories per serving: 269   Fat: 8 grams
Protein: 6 grams   Carbohydrates: 47 grams

CAULIFLOWER CASSEROLE
(Serves 6)

Here's a lowfat main dish you can enjoy during Passover.

1 small head cauliflower
1 onion, chopped
1/4 cup water or vegetable broth
3 large ripe tomatoes, chopped
3 Tablespoons potato starch
1 green pepper, chopped finely
2 carrots, peeled and diced
1 Tablespooon fresh parsley, chopped
Pepper and salt to taste

Divide cauliflower into florets and boil in water until soft. Preheat oven to 350 degrees.

Sauté onion in water or vegetable broth. Add tomatoes and simmer 30 minutes until tomatoes become very soft and you can make a sauce. Stir in potato starch to thicken sauce. Add green pepper, carrots, and parsley, and cook for a few more minutes. Mix well with cooked cauliflower. Pour into casserole dish. Add 3 Tablespoons water. Bake at 350 degrees for 15-20 minutes. Serve warm.

Total calories per serving: 52   Fat: <1 gram
Protein: 2 grams   Carbohydrates: 12 grams

STUFFED EGGPLANT

(Serves 6)

This dish takes a while to prepare but is well worth the effort.

3 medium eggplants, cut lengthwise in half
1 Tablespoon oil
1/4 cup vegetable broth
3 ripe tomatoes, chopped
2 onions, chopped finely
1/2 pound mushrooms, chopped
1/2 cup tomato sauce
Pepper, garlic powder, and salt to taste
2/3 cup raisins (optional)

Peel eggplant. Carve out eggplant leaving 1/2 inch shell all around. Sauté eggplant that has been removed from shell in oil/broth mixture with remaining ingredients until soft, stirring occasionally.

Preheat oven to 375 degrees. Stuff eggplant shells with mixture. Bake covered at 375 degrees for 45 minutes or until shells are soft. Serve warm.

Total calories per serving: 97   Fat: 3 grams
Protein: 3 grams   Carbohydrates: 17 grams

RATATOUILLE
(Serves 5-6)

This is a relatively easy dish to prepare. Serve with mashed potatoes.

1/4 cup water
1 Tablespoon oil
3 ripe tomatoes, cubed
1 large zucchini, diced
1 small eggplant, peeled and cubed
1 large green pepper, diced
1 large onion, chopped
2-3 cloves garlic, minced

In large frying pan sauté all the ingredients over medium heat. Reduce heat and simmer for 15 minutes. Serve warm.

Total calories per serving: 73   Fat: 3 grams
Protein: 2 grams   Carbohydrates: 11 grams

MUSHROOM AND TOMATO BAKE
(Serves 4-5)

This dish tastes great!

1 small onion, chopped finely
2 teaspoons oil
1/2 pound large tomatoes, sliced
1/2 pound mushrooms, chopped finely
2 teaspoons fresh parsley, chopped finely
Pepper and salt to taste
1 pound cooked and mashed potatoes

1/2 cup matzo meal
2 teaspoons margarine

Preheat oven to 350 degrees. Fry onion in oil. Add the sliced tomatoes and mushrooms. Simmer for 10 minutes over a low heat. Add the chopped parsley and seasonings.

Place the mashed potatoes in a lightly oiled large baking dish. Add the mushrooms and tomato mixture. Sprinkle with matzo meal and dot with margarine. Bake at 350 degrees till golden on top.

Total calories per serving: 238   Fat: 5 grams
Protein: 6 grams   Carbohydrates: 45 grams

CHINESE-STYLE STIR FRY
(Serves 8-10)

Here's another delicious Chinese-style dish.

1 pound American or Chinese broccoli, chopped
1 small head of cauliflower, chopped
1/2 bunch scallions, chopped finely
1/2 cup slivered almonds
2 cloves garlic, minced
2 Tablespoons dry red wine
Salt to taste (optional)
2 teaspoons oil
1/3 cup water

Mix together all ingredients and stir fry in pan over high heat, stirring constantly, until cauliflower is tender. Serve warm.

Total calories per serving: 85   Fat: 5 grams
Protein: 4 grams   Carbohydrates: 7 grams

LAYERED VEGETABLE CASSEROLE
(Serves 6)

This dish not only tastes great, but looks beautiful on any table.

1st layer: Pureed root vegetables
4 carrots, peeled and sliced in rounds
2 potatoes, diced
2 turnips, peeled and diced
Pepper to taste
2 Tablespoons margarine

Cook vegetables together in water over medium heat until soft. Drain well. Blend or mash together with pepper and margarine.

2nd layer:
1/2 head small cabbage

Shred cabbage. Cover with water in a small pan. Cook until cabbage is soft and drain.

3rd layer:
1 pound broccoli or cauliflower

Cook one pound of either chopped broccoli or cauliflower in water until soft and drain.

4th layer: Potato croutons
2 large potatoes, peeled
2 teaspoons margarine
Garlic powder, paprika, pepper, and salt to taste

Preheat oven to 300 degrees. Cube potatoes into small pieces. Sauté in margarine until covered with margarine on all sides. Season with garlic powder, paprika, pepper and salt. Spread on cookie sheet and bake at 300 degrees for about 10 minutes, turning occasionally as potatoes begin to brown. Remove from oven.

Raise oven temperature to 350 degrees. In a deep casserole dish, spread in this order: puree, cabbage, broccoli or cauliflower, and then croutons. Bake in a 350 degree oven for 10-15 minutes or until heated through. Serve warm.

Total calories per serving: 211   Fat: 5 grams
Protein: 6 grams   Carbohydrates: 38 grams

INDIAN-STYLE POTATO DISH
(Serves 6)

Here's an absolutely wonderful tasting Indian dish. It is not spicy.

**4 cloves garlic, minced finely
2 teaspoons oil
1 large green pepper, chopped finely
3/4 cup shredded coconut
3 large potatoes, diced
3 ripe tomatoes, chopped finely
Pepper and salt to taste
1-1/2 cups water**

Sauté garlic in oil over medium heat for 1/2 minute. Add pepper and coconut, and lower heat. Add potatoes, tomatoes, seasonings, and water. Bring to a boil and simmer for 40 minutes. Stir occasionally. Serve hot.

Total calories per serving: 202   Fat: 6 grams
Protein: 3 grams   Carbohydrates: 36 grams

VEGETABLE CASSEROLE
(Serves 8)

Here's another lowfat casserole.

4 matzos
3 small ripe tomatoes, chopped
1 onion, chopped finely
1 medium zucchini, grated
2 cups cooked potatoes, cubed
One 10 ounce box frozen spinach, cooked and drained
12 ounce can tomato sauce

Preheat oven to 375 degrees. In a rectangular casserole dish lay 2 pieces of matzo. Then add the following: layer of half the tomatoes, onion, zucchini, potatoes, spinach, and sauce. Repeat layers again, starting with matzo and ending with sauce. Bake 25 minutes at 375 degrees. Serve warm.

Total calories per serving: 125   Fat: 0.5 gram
Protein: 4 grams   Carbohydrates: 28 grams

ZUCCHINI WALNUT CASSEROLE
(Serves 8)

This is a relatively easy casserole to prepare. Serve in moderation.

1 onion, chopped finely
2 pounds zucchini, grated
1/4 pound mushrooms, chopped
1 cup matzo meal

3/4 cup chopped walnuts
Pepper and salt to taste

Preheat oven to 375 degrees. Mix ingredients together well. Press into oiled loaf pan. Bake 45 minutes at 375 degrees. Serve hot or cold.

Total calories per serving: 166   Fat: 7 grams
Protein: 6 grams   Carbohydrates: 22 grams

EGGLESS PASSOVER BLINTZES
(Makes about 8)

Try these unique Passover blintzes. Experiment with different fillings.

3/4 cup matzo meal
1 small banana
1/4 cup potato starch
1-1/4 cups water
4 Tablespoons applesauce (optional)

Blend all ingredients together in blender. Pour about 7 Tablespoons of batter into lightly oiled and preheated frying pan. Cook on medium heat until top is not moist. Scoop out with spatula and place on napkin. If the blintz is breaking, you may not be cooking it long enough. If crisp, you are overcooking.

Preheat oven to 350 degrees. Put some of one of the fillings on the next page (or your own) near the edge of each pancake. Roll pancake and fold ends under. Place in a lightly oiled baking pan with folded ends down. Bake at 350 degrees for a half hour until light brown.

Total calories per unfilled blintz: 83   Fat: 1 gram
Protein: 1 gram   Carbohydrates: 16 grams

FRUIT BLINTZ FILLING
(Serves 4)

This is an absolutely terrific blintz filling!

2 tangerines, peeled and chopped
2 small apples, chopped
1/2 cup each raisins and chopped walnuts (nuts optional)
2/3 cup applesauce
1 teaspoon cinnamon
2 Tablespoons water

Heat ingredients together over medium heat for 15 minutes until apples soften a little. Use as blintz filling.

Total calories per serving: 128   Fat: <1 gram
Protein: 1 gram   Carbohydrates: 34 grams

CHINESE-STYLE BLINTZ FILLING
(Serves 4)

Try this unique blintz filling.

2 carrots, peeled and diced finely
4 mushrooms, chopped
2 stalks celery, chopped
1/2 bunch scallions, chopped finely
3 Tablespoons slivered almonds
1 green pepper or stalk of broccoli, diced (optional)
2 teaspoons oil

1/4 cup water
6 Tablespoons apricot preserves
2 Tablespoons potato starch

Sauté above ingredients, except water, preserves, and starch, in a large frying pan over high heat for 5 minutes. Add water, apricot preserves and potato starch. Heat a few minutes. Use as blintz filling.

Total calories per serving: 173   Fat: 5 grams
Protein: 2 grams   Carbohydrates: 31 grams

STUFFED TOMATOES
(Serves 6)

This dish makes a beautiful centerpiece.

6 large ripe tomatoes
2 teaspoons margarine or oil
3/4 cup matzo farfel or 2 pieces of matzo, crushed
1/2 cup raisins
1 stalk celery, chopped finely
1 Tablespoon dry red wine or tomato juice

Scoop out tomatoes and save pulp. Sauté farfel, raisins, celery, and wine or juice in margarine or oil for 10-15 minutes. Add mixture to pulp and blend well.

Preheat oven to 350 degrees. Stuff tomatoes and place in baking dish. Add 1/2 inch of water on bottom of pan. Bake at 350 degrees for about 15 minutes until tomatoes are tender.

Total calories per serving: 119   Fat: 2 grams
Protein: 2 grams   Carbohydrates: 27 grams

EGGPLANT CASSEROLE
(Serves 6)

Enjoy this delicious casserole dish.

1/3 cup water or vegetable broth
2 teaspoons oil
1 large onion, chopped
1 medium eggplant, peeled and cubed
1/4 cup diced green pepper
11 ounce can tomato and mushroom sauce
1 teaspoon salt (optional)
1/2 teaspoon pepper
2 large tomatoes, diced
1-1/2 cups matzo farfel

Sauté onions in water or broth and oil over medium heat until tender. Add eggplant, green pepper, tomato and mushroom sauce, and seasonings. Cover and cook for 15 minutes or until eggplant is tender. Stir in tomatoes.

Preheat oven to 350 degrees. In a 2-quart baking dish arrange in alternate layers the vegetables and matzo farfel beginning and ending with vegetables. Bake uncovered at 350 degrees for 25 minutes. Serve warm.

Total calories per serving: 134   Fat: 2 grams
Protein: 2 grams   Carbohydrates: 29 grams

STUFFED CABBAGE II

(Serves 6-8)

Here's another delicious stuffed cabbage recipe.

Small head of cabbage
4 teaspoons oil
2 small onions, chopped finely
1-1/2 cups matzo farfel or 4 pieces of matzo crushed
1 cup raisins
2 stalks celery, chopped finely
2 Tablespoons red dry wine (optional)
2/3 cup apple juice
1/2 cup applesauce
29 ounce can tomato sauce
1 cup water

Steam head of cabbage in water until leaves are soft. Remove cabbage from water, cool, and separate leaves.

In oil sauté onions, farfel, raisins, and celery over medium heat for 10 minutes. Add wine, juice, and applesauce. Simmer 5 more minutes.

Preheat oven to 375 degrees. Place some stuffing on each cabbage leaf and fold ends in. Lay in deep baking dish with folded cabbage ends down. Mix tomato sauce with water. Pour sauce over cabbage so leaves remain moist and don't dry out. Bake at 375 degrees for a half hour or until heated through.

Total calories per serving: 268   Fat: 3 grams
Protein: 4 grams   Carbohydrates: 62 grams

EGGPLANT AND POTATO STEW
(Serves 4)

Enjoy this eggplant/potato combination in moderation.

1/2 cup water
2 Tablespoons oil
2 medium onions, sliced
1 medium eggplant, cubed
1 pound potatoes, cubed
28 ounce can tomatoes
Pepper and salt to taste

In pot over medium-high heat sauté onions, eggplant, and potatoes in water/oil mixture for 3 minutes. Stir occasionally. Add remaining ingredients and simmer covered for 20 minutes or until vegetables are tender. Serve warm.

Total calories per serving: 259   Fat: 8 grams
Protein: 6 grams   Carbohydrates: 45 grams

DESSERTS

BAKED FRUIT WITH NUT TOPPING
(Serves 8)

Topping can be served over raw or baked fruit. Eat in moderation.

2/3 cup raisins
1/2 cup hot water
2 apples, chopped
1 cup raw cashews, pine nuts or hazel nuts
1/4 teaspoon cinnamon
8 apples or pears, cored and cut in half lengthwise

Soak raisins in water until soft. Place in blender cup and add remaining ingredients. Blend until creamy. You may have to add some more water. Serve over raw or baked fruit.

Preheat oven to 450 degrees. In pan with water on bottom bake apples or pears at 450 degrees until fruit is soft. Serve with nut topping.

Total calories per serving: 256   Fat: 9 grams
Protein: 3 grams   Carbohydrates: 47 grams

FRUIT KABOBS
(Serves 8)

Children will enjoy this colorful dessert!

2 apples, cubed
2 pears, cubed
2 bananas, peeled and sliced
1/4 pineapple, cubed
1 cup seedless grapes or fresh strawberries

Place the above fruit cubes on 8 skewers alternating fruits and serve.

Total calories per serving: 92   Fat: 1 gram
Protein: 1 gram   Carbohydrates: 24 grams

CINDY'S FRUIT COMPOTE
(Serves 10)

This is a sweet dessert.

2 cups dried peaches, cut in half
2 cups whole pitted dried prunes
2 cups dried apricots
1 cup raisins
2 Tablespoons cinnamon
4 whole cloves (optional)
4 cups apple juice

Simmer above ingredients for one hour. Serve warm. Cold leftovers are also delicious.

Total calories per serving: 273   Fat: 0.5 grams
Protein: 3 grams   Carbohydrates: 72 grams

FRUIT-NUT CHEWS
(Makes 60)

Here's another great treat for children.

2 cups matzo meal
2 cups farfel
1 cup sugar or other sweetner
1 teaspoon cinnamon
1/2 teaspoon ginger powder
1 teaspoon salt
1/2 cup chopped nuts
1 cup raisins or chopped dates
1/4 cup potato starch
1/2 cup oil
1 cup water
1 cup mashed bananas (about 2 large ripe bananas)

Preheat oven to 350 degrees. Combine dry ingredients in a large bowl. Stir in nuts and raisins or chopped dates. Beat potato starch, oil, water, and mashed banana together. Beat into dry mixture.

Drop onto oiled cookie sheets with a teaspoon. Bake at 350 degrees for 20 minutes.

Total calories per cookie: Fat: 2 grams
Protein: 1 gram   Carbohydrates: 12 grams

FROZEN BANANA TREAT

All your guests will enjoy this frozen dessert.

3-4 very ripe bananas, peeled
1/2 cup cocoa
2 Tablespoons water

Place the above ingredients in a blender cup and blend until creamy. Freeze in a container and serve.

Variations: Instead of cocoa try 1/4 cup various fruits. Also, add some dates that have been softened in boiling water beforehand.

Total calories per serving: 153   Fat: 1 gram
Protein: 5 grams   Carbohydrates: 35 grams

APPLE/PEAR PIE
(Serves 8)

Everyone enjoys ending a great meal with pie. Eat in moderation.

Pie Crust: 1/4 cup margarine
2 ripe bananas, peeled and mashed
1 cup matzo meal
2-3 Tablespoons sweetener
1/4 teaspoon cinnamon

Cream above ingredients together. Press into 9-inch pie pan and chill.

Filling: 5 apples, cored and chopped
3 pears, cored and chopped
1/2 cup raisins

Topping: 1/4 teaspoon cinnamon
2 Tablespoons matzo meal
1 Tablespoon chopped nuts

Preheat oven to 375 degrees. Cover apples, pears, and raisins with water in a pot and cook till soft over medium heat. Mix well. Pour into crust. Mix topping ingredients together and sprinkle on top. Bake at 375 degrees for 20-30 minutes. Serve warm or at room temperature.

Total calories per serving: 280   Fat: 7 grams
Protein: 3 grams   Carbohydrates: 55 grams

SWEET POTATO/PINEAPPLE PIE
(Serves 8)

Use above pie crust or your own recipe. Eat in moderation.

Filling:
5 sweet potatoes
20 ounce can juice-pack crushed pineapple, undrained

Bake sweet potatoes. Allow them to cool and then peel off the skins.
   Preheat oven to 325 degrees. Put potatoes in a blender cup with crushed pineapple. Blend till smooth. Pour into shell and bake at 325 degrees for 15 minutes or till heated through. Serve warm or at room temperature.
   Variation: Equivalent amount of fresh chopped pineapple can be substituted for canned pineapple.

Total calories per serving including crust: 247   Fat: 6 grams
Protein: 6 grams   Carbohydrates: 47 grams

FESTIVE MACAROONS 1

(Makes about 20)

These delicious eggless macaroons should be eaten in moderation.

2 cups shredded coconut
4 ripe bananas, mashed
1/4 cup cocoa
1/2 cup walnuts, chopped

Preheat oven to 350 degrees. Blend ingredients together. Form pyramids on a cookie sheet. Bake at 350 degrees for 20 minutes.

Total calories per macaroon: 89   Fat: 5 grams
Protein: 1 gram   Carbohydrates: 11 grams

MACAROONS 11

(Makes about 10)

This is a simple eggless macaroon recipe. Eat in moderation.

1 cup shredded coconut
2 ripe bananas, peeled and mashed

Preheat oven to 350 degrees. Mix ingredients together. Spoon onto oiled baking pan and shape into pyramids. Bake at 350 degrees for 20 minutes.

Total calories per macaroon: 68   Fat: 3 grams
Protein: 1 gram   Carbohydrates: 10 grams

FRUIT BAKE
(Serves 6)

Feel free to experiment with different fruit such as pears and peaches.

1/3 cup water
3 apples, chopped
2/3 cup raisins
1/2 teaspoon cinnamon
1/2 cup walnuts, chopped (optional)
6 ripe small bananas

Preheat oven to 375 degrees. In covered saucepan heat water, apples, raisins, and cinnamon until the apples are soft (5-10 minutes). Remove from heat. Add optional nuts to the mixture and mix well. Slice bananas lengthwise and place half in a loaf pan. Cover with 1/2 the apple mixture. Repeat layers with remaining bananas and apples. Bake for 30 minutes at 375 degrees. Serve warm.

Total calories per serving: 175   Fat: 1 gram
Protein: 2 grams   Carbohydrates: 45 grams

SPICY DATE NUT SPREAD ON MATZO
(Serves 4)

Here's a unique spread to put on matzo during Passover. You can also use it as a cake icing. Use sparingly.

1/4 pound dates, pitted
1/2 cup hot water
1 apple, chopped
1/2 cup walnuts, chopped
1/4 teaspoon cinnamon
Pinch of ginger powder (optional)
4 matzo

Soak dates in hot water for a few minutes. Put mixture in blender cup. Add apple, nuts, and spices. Blend until smooth. Serve on matzo.

Total calories per serving with matzo: 305   Fat: 9 grams
Protein: 7 grams   Carbohydrates: 52 grams

PASSOVER

What holiday is more appropriate to vegetarianism than Passover? What better way to celebrate the coming of spring then with fresh fruits and vegetables? At the seder we call for all those who are hungry to come and join us. Eating lower on the food chain is the first necessary step to reducing world hunger.

Passover is the celebration of our redemption from slavery. Shouldn't we honor G-d's mercy by not promoting the horrible conditions of factory farming and slavery under which animals are raised? As you finish the seder with Chad Gadyu, you may want to think of the words of Philip Pick, founder of the International Jewish Vegetarian Society. "'One only kid my father bought- and a cat came and devoured the kid.' Here is the first act of cruelty and destruction... One crime produces another. Finally, the chain of retribution is stopped by the destruction of the Angel of Death. The moral is that only G-d who gives life can take it away and whether it be human or animal, man has no right or power to do so, if he does, retribution sets in."

Vegetarianism is the first step to ending the chain of violence in this world. It is a personal step each one of us can begin to take this Passover. Hopefully this book will encourage you to become vegetarian all year round.

FAT

J ewish people have grown up on fatty food and love it. If you cook
for the average Westerner, many of your recipes will have to be a
compromise to this acquired taste. However, try very hard to
INCREASE YOUR INTAKE OF RAW OR "PLAIN" STEAMED
FRESH VEGETABLES AND FRUIT. This is the best way to increase
your fiber intake, decrease overconsumption of calories, and lower fat in
your diet.

*Though plant foods do not contain cholesterol, beware that some
vegetables are high in fat, and may contain saturated fat.*

VEGETARIAN FOODS HIGH IN FAT

cheeses, butter, avocado, oil, margarine, nuts, whole milk, coconut,
eggs and mayonnaise

T ry to moderate your use of the above products. If you want to
reduce your fat intake more, sauté in water and bake instead of
frying when possible. Practice moderation in the long run so you
won't be forced to quickly and drastically change your eating patterns due
to illness.

W hen using the recipes in this book, note that some traditional
Passover dishes are high in fat. I've reduced the fat content of
these dishes whenever possible. Remember, this cookbook is
used by people for many different reasons. You should select the recipes
in this book according to the type of diet you are on, your personal needs,
and the advice of your health care provider. Some people will want to use
all the recipes, while others on restricted diets may want to avoid certain
foods. For example, according to your needs, one macaroon may fit into
your diet or it may not.

VEGETARIANISM IN A NUTSHELL

Vegetarianism is the abstinence from meat, fish and fowl. Among the many reasons for being a vegetarian are compassion for animals, aesthetic considerations, ecological and hunger concerns, economic, religious or spiritual, and health reasons. The American Dietetic Association has affirmed that a vegetarian diet can meet all known nutrient needs. LIKE EVERY DIET, THE KEY TO A HEALTHY VEGETARIAN DIET IS SIMPLE. Eat a variety of foods, including lots of dark green leafy vegetables, and have high-fat, high-salt, empty-calorie foods be only a small part of your diet.

PROTEIN

As long as sufficient calories are consumed daily, protein needs can easily be met by all healthy vegetarians. Protein and vegetarianism was first closely analyzed for the public in *Diet For A Small Planet*, by Frances Moore Lappe'. Although this book introduced many important vegetarian concepts, the theory of complementing proteins proved to be misleading, and was later revoked by the author in an updated edition.

In using the concept of limiting amino acids, many people wrongly assumed this meant there was none of that amino acid in the food. In fact, most foods contain at least some of all essential amino acids. Exceptions are some fruits and empty calorie or junk foods.

Another important fact is that the body maintains a relatively constant supply of essential amino acids in what is called the amino acid pool. This pool is made up of amino acids from endogenous sources (digestive secretions and desquamated cells) with only a small portion coming from diet. The ability of the body to recycle amino acids reassures us that essential amino acids do not have to be eaten in any specific pattern of mealtime or type of food.

Again, the points to remember are consume a variety of wholesome foods, including some protein-rich foods and consume sufficient calories.

VEGANISM

Vegetarianism is the abstinence of meat, fish and fowl. Veganism is trying not to use other animal products and by-products such as eggs, dairy products, leather, wool, most soaps and toothpastes which contain lard, etc.

A vegan may abstain from eggs or dairy for health or ethical reasons. Though no direct killing results from eating eggs or dairy, a vegan feels he or she is promoting the meat industry by consuming these products. Once the animals are too old to be productive, they are sold as meat. Male chickens and calves are not useful, so they are also sold to the butcher or soap factory. Many people stay away from these products because of cruel factory farm conditions associated with their production.

RABBIS WHO SUPPORT OR ARE (WERE) VEGETARIAN

Rabbi David Cohen

Rabbi Shear Yashuv Cohen: Chief Rabbi of Haifa

Rabbi Shlomo Goren: Ashkenazic Chief Rabbi of Israel

Rabbi Abraham Isaac Kook (Kuk)

Rabbi David Rosen: Former Chief Rabbi of Ireland now living in Israel

SOME FAMOUS JEWISH VEGETARIANS

Shmuel Yosef Agnon: Modern Hebrew fiction writer who won the Nobel Prize in Literature in 1966.

Albert Einstein: Theory of relativity.

Franz Kafka: Novelist.

Isaac Bashevis Singer: Writer who won the Nobel Prize for Literature in 1978.

BIBLIOGRAPHY

Akers, Keith. *A Vegetarian Sourcebook*, Vegetarian Press, 1993.

"Position of The American Dietetic Association: Vegetarian Diets," *Journal of The American Dietetic Association*, November, 1993.

Berman, Louis. *Vegetarianism and Jewish Tradition*, Ktav, 1981.

Robertson, Laurel; Flinders, Carol; Ruppenthal, Brian. *The New Laurel's Kitchen*, Ten Speed Press, 1986. Good vegetarian nutrition section.

Schwartz, Richard. *Judaism and Vegetarianism*, Micah Publications, 1988.

Tree of Life, An Anthology of Articles Appearing in The Jewish Vegetarian, A.S. Barnes and Co., 1977.

United States Department of Agriculture Home and Garden Bulletin Number 72 Nutritive Value of Foods. In most libraries.

Wasserman, Debra. *The Lowfat Jewish Vegetarian Cookbook*, The Vegetarian Resource Group, 1994.

Wasserman, Debra; Mangels, Reed. *Simply Vegan*, 2nd edition, The Vegetarian Resource Group, 1995. Great vegan nutrition section.

INFORMATION ON LOCAL JEWISH VEGETARIAN GROUPS IN THE UNITED STATES:

The Vegetarian Resource Group, PO Box 1463, Baltimore, Maryland 21203

OTHER BOOKS FROM THE VEGETARIAN RESOURCE GROUP

If you are interested in purchasing any of the following VRG titles, please send a check or money order made out to *The Vegetarian Resource Group*, (Maryland residents must add 5% sales tax) and mail it along with your order to: *The Vegetarian Resource Group, P.O. Box 1463, Baltimore, MD 21203*. Make sure you include your shipping address. Or call (410) 366-VEGE to order with a Visa or Mastercard credit card. Price given includes postage in the United States. Outside the USA please pay in US funds by credit card or money order and add $2.00 per book for postage.

THE LOWFAT JEWISH VEGETARIAN COOKBOOK
Healthy Traditions From Around The World
By Debra Wasserman

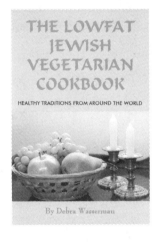

The Lowfat Jewish Vegetarian Cookbook contains over 150 lowfat, vegan international recipes. Savor potato knishes, Polish plum and rhubarb soup, Indian curry and rice, Greek pastries, and Spinach Pies. Feast on Romanian apricot dumplings, North African barley pudding, Pumpernickel and Russian flat bread, sweet fruit kugel, Czechoslovakian noodles with poppy seeds, and Russian blini. Celebrate with eggless challah, hamentashen for Purim, Chanukah latkes, mock chopped "liver," Russian charoset, eggless matzo balls, and Syrian wheat pudding.

Breakfast, lunch, and dinner menus are provided, as well as 33 unique Passover dishes and Seder ideas, and Rosh Hashanah Dinner suggestions. Each recipe is accompanied by a nutritional analysis.
TRADE PAPERBACK $15

SIMPLY VEGAN

Quick Vegetarian Meals, 2nd Edition
By Debra Wasserman &
Reed Mangels, Ph.D., R.D.

Simply Vegan is an easy-to-use
vegetarian guide that contains over
160 kitchen-tested vegan recipes.
Each recipe is accompanied by a
nutritional analysis.

Reed Mangels, Ph.D., R.D., has included an extensive vegan nutrition
section on topics such as Protein, Fat, Calcium, Iron, Vitamin B12,
Pregnancy and the Vegan Diet, Feeding Vegan Children, and Calories,
Weight Gain, and Weight Loss. A Nutrition Glossary is provided, along
with sample menus, meal plans, and a list of the top recipes for iron,
calcium, and Vitamin C.

Also featured are food definitions and origins, and a comprehensive list
of mail-order companies that specialize in selling vegan food, natural
clothing, cruelty-free cosmetics, and ecological household products.
TRADE PAPERBACK $13

MEATLESS MEALS
FOR WORKING PEOPLE

Quick & Easy Vegetarian Recipes
By Debra Wasserman & Charles Stahler

Meatless Meals For Working People is the
perfect book for new vegetarians. It contains
over 100 delicious fast and easy recipes, plus
ideas which teach you how to be a vegetarian
within your hectic schedule using common convenient vegetarian foods.
This handy guide also contains a spice chart, party ideas, information on
fast food chains, and much, much more.
TRADE PAPERBACK $6

VEGETARIAN JOURNAL'S GUIDE TO NATURAL FOODS RESTAURANTS IN THE U.S. & CANADA

OVER 2,000 LISTINGS OF RESTAURANTS & VACATION SPOTS
For the health-conscious traveler, this is the perfect traveling companion
to insure a great meal or the ideal lodgings when away from home or if
you are looking for a nearby vegetarian place.

The Vegetarian Journal's Guide to Natural Foods Restaurants
(Avery Publishing Group, Inc.) is a helpful guide listing eateries state by
state and province by province. Each entry not only describes the house
specialties, varieties of cuisine, and special dietary menus, but also includes
information on ambiance, attire, and reservations. It even tells you
whether or not you can pay by credit card. And there's more. Included
in this guide are listings of vegetarian inns, spas, camps, tours, travel
agencies, and vacations spots. **TRADE PAPERBACK $13**

SIMPLE, LOWFAT & VEGETARIAN

By Suzanne Havala, M.S., R.D. and Mary Clifford, R.D.

This 368-page book is an easy-to-use guide to lowfat eating that shows
you how to reduce the fat in your meals with a few simple changes, but
allows you to continue enjoying dining in Chinese, Mexican, fast food,
Indian, natural foods, and other restaurants. You'll also learn what to
order when flying, traveling on Amtrak, going to the movies, or visiting
an amusement park. Good food choices, before and after menu magic, fat
content of foods, and helpful charts are presented for these and many
other situations. **Simple, Lowfat & Vegetarian** also contains 30 days of
quick lowfat meals, tips on how to modify your own recipes, sample
menus, weekly shopping lists, plus 50 vegan recipes.
TRADE PAPERBACK $15

INDEX

To order additional copies of
NO CHOLESTEROL
PASSOVER RECIPES
send $10 (including postage) per book
to The Vegetarian Resource Group,
PO Box 1463, Baltimore, MD 21203.

To Join
The Vegetarian
Resource Group
and Receive the Bimonthly
Vegetarian Journal
for One Year Send $20.00 to
The Vegetarian Resource Group,
PO Box 1463,
Baltimore, MD 21203.

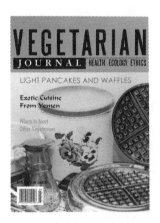